Beyond Basilicas

www.chuckoneilauthor.com

Beyond Basilicas

ISBN: 978-1-957883-18-2 (paperback)
ISBN: 978-1-7362517-4-4 (e book)
Library of Congress Control Number: 2021901062

Cover Art: 'The Green Mountains,' Edgar O. Miner, circa 1950

StoneBear Publishing LLC - 01/2021
Milford, PA 18337
www.stonebearpublishing.com

by Chuck O'Neil

Holding Things Together

Beyond Basilicas

Eating Out

The Perfect Scar

SAWKILL FALLS EDITIONS

The Falls of the Sawkill
19th Century
Artist: Signature Illegible

for Celeste

for Ben, Chuck, Beth, Sarah

BEYOND BASILICAS

Chuck O'Neil

CONTENTS

5

BEYOND BASILICAS

Make your own bible. Select and collect all the words and sentences that in all your readings have been to you like the blast of a trumpet.

Emerson

Preamble

We
The people with scratchpads
And apparitions

With pigment
And picture windows

In order to form
More perfect unions
In order to navigate the dark hours
And diminish our confusion

Ordain this day
To lay up stone walls
Grow roses
Fire clay
Hammer copper
If that's what it takes

Because
She's full of grace
Who brings forth with her own eyes

He every morning's
A prisoner released
Who names his own angels

1

Among your earthiest words, angels stray . . .

Patrick Kavanagh

Weeknight in Winter

Our balcony flag slapped
Like sailcloth much of the night

Spluttering so ceaselessly
We could imagine its stripes
Blown off by morning

The trees heaved
Our second story shook
Snow came from east of us

And we supposed this was
What it was like to be alive

In Februarys
When the wind held nothing back
When snow fell at will

When ancestors would batten drafty windows
And blanket themselves
And outsleep howling in the eaves
Splatterings against the glass

Or alone   or in pairs   lie low
Wide-eyed   all ears
As though stowed below decks
In heavy seas

Digging Out

A man can be
Shoveling his sidewalk
After a daylong snow   spreading salt
As if any visitor would arrive so late
Wondering about the path he's unburying
The snow he heaves off
The way others heaved it off

When his father's brother comes to him
The one who called his own shots around town
Had a K of C hall named in his honor
And a picture taken with the pope
The one the ice laid out winters ago
Just a few feet from his front stoop

Keep your nose clean   son   he says
And all the balls in the air
Makin' sure your own
Aren't the ones gettin' juggled

You're an Irishman
You'll do fine down here

Plow scraping across town
Night sky flung full of glitter
Snow thigh-high all around him

Even Russia comes on a night like this
Mandelstam   Akhmatova
Both shoveling walkways laced with ice
Digging out under the frigid fever of stars

Heaven on Earth

All the boys in school
Said the same thing
What a waste

She was way too beautiful
To be a nun

Her French class was full of boys
Who   when getting up from their desks
Had to cover themselves with textbooks

Though   truthfully
That stiffness in those days
Seemed for the most part involuntary

It could even happen
Studying theorems and proofs
In hairy Mr. Pappas's geometry class

While we spent the summer trying
To keep our reflexive hypotenuses in check
We were crushed to learn that Sister Laura
Wouldn't be back to teach French III

She and Father Brendan (our principal)
Had fallen in love backstage while
Working on last spring's musical

They'd given up their marriages to Christ
Is the way we heard it
And exchanged vows
On a sloop in the Sound

We could see her sailing away with him
Out of our lives forever
Hugging the coast
South past Cape Hatteras
Down body and soul
Into the simmering Florida Keys

Missionaries of passion
Everything out-of-this-world
We believed back then of earthly love
Hepburn and Tracy

Woman in the Window

The basket between the columns
Topples with scarlet
Sways in the lake breeze

A hummingbird hovers
Kisses   startles
Rekisses   vanishes

The woman in the window
Witnesses everything
Remembering in the lessening light

How she dared him
After school
With her upturned flowering mouth

How he kissed her quick
And flew off
Across Spring Garden Avenue

Night

A sliver of a moon
Hung above the river

The river's ink flowing south
Under a hundred bridges

Downstairs in the kitchen
Ants worship a peach pit

One of us left by the sink
And are numbed by its sweetness

It won't always be like this
The refrigerator's familiar hum

Everyone we love
Sleeping in a single time zone

Our arms lifting so easily
Like wings off the cove

Key to the House

We'd keep it hidden among stones
And for our own use

We'd work the kerfed brass
Into the door at all hours

Now   feeling in darkness
For the right key on a ring full of keys

Fingers may skim the chimney's
Nubbed rubble skin again

Any one of us may come
Tumbling a lock

Standing suddenly stock-still
Listening at the threshold for voices

2

We grow more candid as we grow up.
There is fate to thank for that.
And changes in life coincide
With major changes in ourselves.

Yevtushenko

Trans. Albert C. Todd

Backstory

1
In the year of my birth
The pope cleared his throat
And spoke out across the frigid basilica
Echoing the gold and stone
Leaving no doubt when he was done
About the Blessed Mother's bodily rise

Meanwhile   cooped up
Above a flower shop in Queens
Kerouac rolled the scroll
Of his own assumptions

As McCarthy cooked up his list of communists
And war flared in Korea
And Truman gave imprimatur to the H-bomb

Sinatra went to #5 singing *Goodnight Irene*
And Merton split the scene long before
Busing himself off
To the Trappists in Kentucky

By the end of that decade
My report card came home with all +'s
My height 51-1/4, my weight 59-1/2

I was never 'tardy'   never dismissed
And my citizenship that year was 'satisfactory'
The best of two available grades

In a handwritten note nibbed in blue ink
Miss Lafontaine said she
Enjoyed having me in her room
She'd read to us during disaster drills
Each of us tucked under a desk

In Social Studies
It was the year the flags changed
Alaska (igloos   white bears   tundra)
Hawaii (coconuts   Captain Cook   volcanic rock)
Becoming our 49th and 50th States

In the dead of night
Somebody called Dalai Lama
Hightails the Himalayas out of Tibet

In broad daylight
Somebody called Castro
Rumbles through the streets of Havana

A UFO glows over 5th Avenue
As its architect's lowered to his rest

Marilyn Monroe plays Sugar Cane
A fine snow dusts the Iowa field
Where a plane carrying musicians crashed

And on June 16th 1959
I'm promoted to Miss Clay's fourth grade class

2
It was the year our father (the second of eight)
Who'd left school at fifteen
Who was blessed
With good hands and good brains
Was finishing the brick house
He'd built for us on two lots

Where our earthly mother
(Herself the seventh of eight)
Whose parents spoke mostly Polish
Whose own schooling ended early
And who too was blessed
With good hands and good brains
Would remake our home each day

And the two of them
Raised four on one workingman's wages
In the East Great Plains section of the city
West of the river
Where the downtown stood with all its stores

And we lived in those days
Where there were fields
One   in a valley
With a stream threading through it
Was torched each fall
And flooded for skating

The whole town would skate there
Under the lights

We took our cues from older boys
Who'd smoke in the lean-to
And skate circles around the girls

Another field behind our house had horses

3
And everybody did the best they could
And some things   we suspected
Were less than perfect

One Sunday   the visiting Franciscan
Told us we'd *lucked out*
Born as we were
Into the One True Church

Saying rosaries as we were
For the Russians
Offering Novenas as we were
For Protestants   atheists   Jews   and the like
Digging down deep as we were
For the second collection

And word of mouth crisscrossed
From house to house
As rotary phones dozed on hall tables

And there were days of obligation
Nights when the great pearl face of the moon
Hung above the trees

It was Revelation one minute
Guesswork the next
Times when our clocks stopped altogether
As when we watched a friend's father
For who-knows-how-long
Hammering straight a can full of bent nails
Making Christians out of 'em   he said
Peering up over his glasses

20

Or the morning that went on without end
When we heard
Our Grandma's heart had given out

Time when Ike
Practiced his putting in the oval office
Shuffled off advisors to Southeast Asia
Crusaded for the creation
Of turnpikes from sea to shining sea

4

And though most of us in those days
Got where we were going
With time to spare
Surveyors came to get the lay of the land

And it wasn't long
Till turnpikes sliced the counties
And one highway begat another
And their exits spidered off
And jughandled and cloverleafed
And intercoursed with our older roads

And we burrowed
And built bridges   seventy times seven
And named them with the names
Of influential men

And not without our hopes
We went out far on our new roads
Cruising the arteries and connectors
And we drove more as the crow flew

John the XXIII
Our new Peter of Rome
Conclaved his Cardinals

Together they hemmed and hawed
But somehow in the end
Divined God's intentions for the rest of us

Speaking in His absence
They mandated that altars rotate
And that Mea Culpas and Dominus Vobiscums
Be spoken in the local tongue

And soon from the pews
Parishioners cleared their throats
And priest and flock were face to face
And together traded holy vernaculars

Some souls fingered beads
During the new guitar Mass
Muttering rosaries for dear life
But most queued up
And took the bread and sipped the cup

And all at once women were released
From covering their heads
And Fridays were emancipated from fish

And it wasn't long after that
That rotary phones begat touch-tone

5
And the sun rose and the sun went down
And the news in those days
Was not all bad
Though   as turnpikes sliced the counties
So they slit the cities

And stores drained out into the fields
And called themselves Plazas
Shopping Centers   Galleries   Malls

And turnpikes called themselves
Interstates   Highways   Parkways
Expressways   Beltways   Throughways
Even sometimes Freeways

And the sons of men
Rode in the driver's seat
And like their forefathers
Made the most of their assumptions

Around this time
Some of the boulevards   parks
Stadiums and the like   were christened
With the initials of assassinated males

Around this time
The attack in the Gulf of Tonkin was concocted

Lady Bird chirps *Keep America Beautiful*
And crusades coast to coast
Against billboards and turnpike trash

Merton's shocked to kingdom Come
In a bathtub in Bangkok
(Too curious for his own good
Some Church Fathers murmur)

Napalm scorches the fields   torches the hootches
A killer-dust drifts down
Death-misting the jungles and the rivers

On the news we see monks in flames
Bags swollen with corpses
Boxes draped with flags

That summer before sophomore year
In the swelter of the basement
Of the brick block-long velvet factory

(A fixture forever in our town about to
Slam-shut and head south a thousand miles)
I dunk and hoist reels of expensive fabric
In the stink and steam of the dye room

And Steve McQueen
Squeals the streets of San Francisco

NASA shoots the moon
Light-years ahead of the Russians

And in a marinated field in Upstate New York
Santana scalds
A long version of *Soul Sacrifice*
And the Band hammers home *The Weight*

6
And one generation passed
And another one came
And one thing led to another

Before long   we kibitz cordlessly
From our porches and backyards
Rome fiddles with semantics
As the proclivities of certain clergy
Come to light

Blue laws loosen
Speed limits lift as highways gyre out
As throughways sprout their express lanes
As life   the living of it one day to the next
Gets less affordable somehow
Even as incomes couple
Even while offspring diminish

And new fathers   new mothers
Do what they have to do
To hold their own   strapped in many of them
Before the crows caw
Flocking entrance ramps   flying freeways
Braking heavily and funneling down
Saint Christopher velcroed to a dashboard
Rosary dangling from a rear view
Radios cranked   red white and blue
Tattering antennas in the dawn's early light

And we shop
On the old days of rest
Roll dice in the unreal cities

Suddenly phones fold up
And slip into purses and vibrate thighs

Towers collapse

One old pope dies
And another old pope
Pops up in his place

Evangelists insist these are
At long last   the last days

Politicians promise
Statisticians reminisce

A few choose Chekhov
Fewer still Camus

And some are sorry to say
It could be true
That nothing's new under the sun
That things'll get fair
Only in the next life

Yet others
Others on long commutes
Come to see just how
Good news becomes no news at all
How   above the fold
Even in a little hill town paper
News sources lead
With what breeds hopelessness

See how no camera crew
Assembles this spring afternoon
When the yellow bus draws up
Under the wide maples
Their rust-colored buds about to burst

See how many miracles are missed
One after another
As grade school sons and daughters
Step down with their backpacks
Carrying their coats

Vanity of vanities
See how no pollster shows up
To total the souls
Who call out from their steering wheels
For the safekeeping of these least ones

To Yahweh   to the Risen Christ
To Allah   to Vishnu
To the gods of cul-de-sacs
To angels of intersections
And alleys and avenues

Citizen-saints who live in the world
Who go one holy moment to the next
Mostly unnoticed
By the powers and principalities that be

Who do their jobs
Who pray more or less breath by breath
Beyond basilicas
Barely moving their lips

3

For the ones who survived

Beachheads   deserts   mountains   jungles

But were lost in the battle

Of their hometown returns

Memorial Days

1
The Saints we were called

I feel the thick sticks in my hands still
Rimshots and paradiddles popping off
The snare into that blue
Connecticut milltown morning air

Tom-toms answering one row back
My brother blowing trumpet
In the brass section
Fifty-star flags lining our route

And marshaled in behind us
The Veterans of Foreign Wars
Boy and Girl Scouts   antique cars
A politician in the back seat
Of a lustrous old Buick
Flicking his candy to kids in the street

Radiating-red and polished chrome fire trucks
Police   sirens off   roof lights
Flipping and reflecting in the storefront glass

It was all I could do back then

To keep from tripping over myself
Lovestruck as I was
For a girl in the color guard

She was going with our team's
Star running back
Who everyone said was headed
For the first string of some
Powerhouse Catholic college

Soon he'd be gone
Gunning for a bowl game
She'd have to notice me then
Marching not fifteen feet from her

2

New hometown
A hundred towns west
Of my old hometown
And decades since the B-movie
Of my high school days

Roads   lawns   monuments nearly dry
After last night's rain

New parade day   new youth
Fresh-faced   mostly in step

Trumpeting and drumming a march
Cooked up from a pop song
Ratamacues and ghost notes
Echoing our little canyon of historic buildings

And falling in as before
The civic organizations
Keepers of Commonwealth law
Rescuers   volunteers
Veterans of our most recent wars

We all marvel at the vintage cars
Washed and waxed
Pacing behind the bagpipers
Down the center of Broad Street

It's easy to see
How a country can come to sing
A catchy jingle
See the USA
In your Chevrolet

We the people   onlookers
From sidewalks and gutters
Seated in folding chairs
Know the black and white of it

And standing in shade

Beneath the court house beech tree
Recollect those
Who'd have lived whole lives here

Citizens like ourselves
Attending high school winter tournaments
Watching offspring run   shoot
Rebound and dribble

But were called up
And answering the call
Left this kingdom
Of feeder streams and waterfalls
For all time

3

The veterans march to Memorial Park
And mark time
And stand at attention
And under the arching maples go
Silent to honor the dead
Some of them
From the old school on Harford Street

Some from the 58,000 of my generation
Brothers long-gone with their unborn children
Remembered now as the fifty-star flag

Exhales   snaps and sags its shoulders
As   at half-staff   the black and white
Of the still-missing
Lifts once and goes limp

Gone   the running back who enlisted
Gone   Warriors and Saints
Whose numbers came up

Gone   the politician flicking his candy
Gone   the black and white of the first TV's
Gone   replaced with
Less-menacing-looking facilities
The old brick munitions factories

And   dead themselves
Ancient history in fact
To most of those
Assembling around war memorials

Presidents who plead the oath
And misled
And kept our small-town graveyards fed

Gone too   the inventors of the last century
Gone to dust   its engineers   its charioteers

Though on black and white balloon tires
Some of the stunning
Monstrosities they designed
Roll before our eyes
Spit-shined
Hearse-like in the blinding sun

For Howie

and for Celeste's brother   Stephen

Johnson lied and Nixon
Widened the war into Cambodia

Kids my age
Got their heads bashed in Chicago

And peace activists on campus
Were up in arms
When the college gave up
A few rooms in my dorm
To help some guys
Returning from Nam

Vets who'd made it
Out of the jungles alive   they protested
Ought to be able to survive on their own
In downtown Providence

My dorm's location
Situated as it was on mental hospital grounds
Meant none of them would have
Far to go if things got a little crazy

Of the vets who got rooms in Chapin Hall
I only remember Howie now

He was the lone black guy in our dorm
Except for the Center
On our nationally-ranked basketball team
Who dunked with such ferocity
He broke a backboard

He was trailed by his entourage
As he ducked under doorways
And had everybody looking the other way
When a cloud of reefer smoke
Would fill his end of the hall
He lived among us just a few months
Before some alum got him a car
And a place of his own

Howie   back from the war just a month
Poked his dark face into my room
To see which white boy
Was blasting James Brown

To explain myself
I said I was a drummer on weekends
He fired back that he'd been
Doin' time shootin' gooks

And added with a smirk
Right   you rip off our music
We fight your war

He took to calling me Ginger
After Cream's drummer   Ginger Baker
I took to calling him Howitzer
After the guns displayed
On our campus Quad by the ROTC
And it seemed to me we became friends

Once   when I lay in bed for days
He felt my head to check for fever
And said it was probably
Some *goddamn Asian flu*
Sergeant that he was
He said I would be OK
And by the end of the week I was

But I'd never open his door
Without knocking first
After the time he hurled
A knife at my head

Thought you was a gook   he slurred
And buried his grin
Back into the bag

He'd been breathing into
Which filled and collapsed
With each of his heavy breaths
The brown paper crushing
And uncrushing like a party favor

His room reeked of modeling cement
Was dark most days
Had no music playing

It wasn't possible
To touch his head and tell him
Just some godamn flu

By Thanksgiving break
He'd driven off
In his oil-burning Impala
Muffler spluttering down Eaton Street
Like ammunition shooting up the neighborhood

Tossing the Globe

So much of the old life
The borders   the enemies you guarded against
Are all history now

Only the seas seem accurate
The lakes
Those thin blue rivers

True
Your globe is out-of-round
And should be disposed of

But first
Spin it on your finger
Like a Globetrotter

Hear yourself whistling
Or humming if you can't whistle
Sweet Georgia Brown

Spread your shooting hand
Along the mottled ridge
Of a favorite mountain range

Imagine stepping back
Behind the three-point line
Launching the game-winner

Whisper *Adios* to phantom regimes
And to all those
You've been keeping prisoner

As the planet finger-rolls
Into the trash
Say *Sayonara* to a world without bounce

Approaching All Souls' Day

Standing by the end of the driveway
At dusk

The man pokes his rake
Into a leaf pile

And   remembering their names
Stirs up smoke

Incense
Flames

Red-letter Days

In the ash   high as the house is now
Blue jays are making a nest

They could've settled
In a more established maple
Or one of those uniquely-limbed
Kentucky coffeetrees

Yet fitting they should pick
A branch here in town
In the thick of it

Because a jay has little kinship
With birds that soar above the river
Or roost like Hollywood-types
In the tips of high-hilled hickories

No affiliation with that gorgeous white one
Some poets write about
Floating across a mirror lake
Like the paraclete himself
And making just the right splash

Beady-eyed survivors
Blue jays take nobody's word as gospel

Are practical as Unitarians in matters of belief
Probably have (as all winged creatures must)
A concern or two about the hereafter

But now   jinking the yard for materials
They're consumed with nestbuilding
In   of all places   that sapling
You stood in a hole one night after work
Thousands of days ago
And backfilled
And kept from nicking with the mower
And watered a little in the beginning
But otherwise let go

You're tempted on a morning like this
When trees lift leaves and sway
To believe in halcyon days again
That somehow   in the face of all you know
About chaos and creaturehood
These high   breezy   sun-soaked days
Could be your red-letter days

So weary are you now
Of dousing everything with doubt
So great is your desire for equilibrium
Wings

4

Out of Body

Lovers love this slow shift
Of dusk into darkness

Lights out throughout the house
The moon sheens the snow

And shines in the undressed window
Spills over pictures of ancestors

Over the chest of drawers
Across the sloped ceiling   the bed

The bodies on the bed
Interwoven now   aglow

Lovers can go missing in light like this
Spirited off to a mountain town

Or a fishing village
Pitched on a foreign coast

The Hours

From midnight on snow pelts the sash
Every road's closed by morning

The snow's so deep
We can imagine ourselves

Miles from the nearest neighbor
In a North Kingdom farmhouse

I love our isolation   and your voice
Calling me down to the fireplace

All these years and we love
The way we move around each other

So let snow overwhelm the driveway
Let somebody declare a state of emergency

For all the hours of disaster
Let us be the only two souls in town

Going Left

Most mornings   like clockwork
The man with the sick wife
Drives himself a mile and a half
To the wooden store
A stone's throw from the state line

It would make sense for him
To be more like his neighbors
Who have their papers delivered before dawn
By a banged-up Honda
Blinking light atop its roof
Like some emergency vehicle
Flanneled arm stuffing
The yawning yellow mouths
At the ends of driveways

But then   you wouldn't be praying just now
(If a flicker of goodwill
Can be counted for prayer)
Seeing him so early
Steering out among the steaming fields
Blackbirds clustering up and collapsing
Two blue herons squawking

Toward the lake's west shore

Or that other daybreak
When he stopped at the bottom of the hill
And sat a second before going left

Coasting Jacobs Road
The way a mate-for-life
River bird might lift
And float out over water for a time
Before circling back
And feathering the gravity down to earth

Headline

Boston   1861
He thinks he would've lived here then
Owner of a struggling
Sole proprietorship   no doubt

Walking Boylston in a fog of payables
When the news catches up with him
Not about the republic
Early at war with itself

Cambridge   out on Brattle Street
He imagines the famous poet
The one who wrote *Psalm of Life*
Racing from his study

His wife's dress having caught fire
Wrapping her in a rug
Rolling with her
On the parlor floor

On his own for the afternoon
(*His* wife at a conference
In one of the tall hotels)
The man has benched himself

In the Public Garden
Away from the ticker-taping television
And the good-looking anchorwoman
Naming the lame

Traffic moans the Common
Leaves above him all in flames
Some buried news
From across the river weighs in

When the world
Knew less about fire
Tragedy   he guesses
Was mainly a private matter

And quatrains more relied upon
Even pigeons would've hummed hymns
Back then   bobbing the walkways
Maintaining their Victorian distances

Accident

Police lights gyrating   two troopers
One motioning to rubberneckers
The other establishing his hat
Lifting his pistol
Crossing toward the black bear
Writhing on the embankment

No blood anywhere
He must've spun the windshield
And tumbled the culvert to end up up there

You have misgivings
About the Karma theory of collisions
But consider   as you brake-and–roll
Past the totaled Corolla
Just who the bear could become in his next life
A chef   Park Ranger
A keeper of bees with a lust for honey

As best you can figure
Through the stubborn sun glare
Nobody   given our hemisphere
And time of year   seems all that surprised
Not the tow truck driver anyway

Motorists crawl nose-to-bumper
Along this hilly stretch
Most of them like you
Hungry   headed home   needing to pee
But feeling they'd gotten off easy

Considering those chosen for the crash scene
A mother and her preschool-aged son
Huddled near the guardrail   transfixed
By the massive brother from the woods
With such tragic timing

Who'd been fattening for his winter sleep
Who drools   lolls   and appears now
To have howled his last
Why-hast-thou-forsaken-me
As the officer with the gun
Hops the buckled shoulder and hoofs it
Through the loosestrife and stiff grass

He's awfully young (baby-faced almost)
And in your rear view looks new
To roadside works of mercy
The way he hesitates   then shoots the bear
Once in the head
Once for good measure in the chest

The Eagle

for Ben

You were there
The day I shot the eagle

Still in my boots
Out on that workingman's
Nine-holer by the Delaware

Clocking it through the frizzled fairways
Bunkers stiff as mortar mix
Greens pebble-gritted
Peppered with goose dung

I feel the *thwick!* of the eight-iron
The ringed range ball squeezing
Off the end of the club

We chatter at it
Get up   Hurry ball
Left   Be Left
It plops-runs-hits-the-pin-and-drops

I throw my club in the air
Like a Watson or an Irwin

You   firstborn   caddying for me
Not yet in your teens
Have never seen your father
So afflicted with joy before

You go wild with me
As we race to the flag
Our whoops and yells woven together
Carrying the river
Echoing the cliffs

Checkup

All in one motion the dentist
Stands-strips-his-gloves-congratulates

Cavity-free   gums in great shape
X-rays auguring well for the future
See you in six months   he calls back
On his way to another mouth down the hall

Relieved   music from the old days
Wafting the office   waiting only
For the gentle hygienist now

Not the worst thing in the world
To sit in a dentist's chair
With so wide a window on the river

Water birds in migration
Above the metal-webbed bridge
Cars glinting across from one state
To another   city lights yellowing-up

Lucky to have what's left of the daylight
On a moon-tinged Indian summer afternoon
Lucky to catch the last blue canoes

The last orange life jackets
The last few faces on the water

And blessed somehow too
To be heartbroken again
Remembering with the last flashes of sun
The boy who slipped on snow
And slid from the cliffs
To the ice-chunked river below

How with no drill shrilling a molar
With such letter-perfect weather
(No snow   no ice-laced ledges to curse)
The river roiling without guile
Through the eel traps
Baptizing beaches and bridge pilings
Eddying and swirling south
How to account for such a grief-blessing

And what grace is it that visits river-watchers
What mists above the rapids and the rocks
What fathoming passes through glass
As daylight dies
And darkness dials in

Watering Can

Memory the way it is now
I go rummaging for answers
Among catalogs   binders
Drawings of old projects

And see behind some flooring samples
A watering can   its spout
Slender as the stem of a day lily

I can't account for its presence
In a business like this
Where the only plants are long-fallen
Trunks of hardwoods
Sawn up for millwork and cabinetry

An hour goes by at least
I'm figuring a decent-sized job
On East 10th Street when

Looking up from a detail
I see him coming into my office
Unscheduled as always
(He loves to keep me guessing)

Handsome as ever in his early twenties
Captain of his crew team
Agnostic or atheist majoring in religion
Haunting the theater and film departments

He stops by   he says   *just to say Hi*
Juggling a pot of ivy in each hand
Variegated   lush   cascading

My son   delivering to me
The dappled green of his hope that morning
And tucked under his arm
The slim can he'll leave for soaking its soil

Reception

The father of the bride stood
And apologized
He was no joke teller
No public speaker   he said
And these days
A reluctant pontificator as well
Besides   they knew already
All they needed to know
He had his hopes for them though

Some under the great tent shifted
When he started with a wish for
Transubstantiation
(*For lack of a better word*   he said)
Of the daily details
Juiced from time to time
With a shot of insurrection
To fend off glossy things
Men so often peddle as indispensable

For the children
He had a wish they'd be taught
To steady themselves in the wind
Study signs

Like a broad-winged hawk
On a sycamore limb

Wheeling the orchard
Walled fields   the cemetery
She elevates   plummets
All the while reeling in her prey

He hoped   as first teachers
Their parents would live
With a love of the afternoon
Its slow drift through trees and streets

And morning as the rise
From the dead it actually is

A lifelong love of any hour as
Phenomenal   unrepeatable   a gift

Never give up on your kids   he said
Never give up on your kids

Earth means to mend itself
Increase its lakewaters of grace

And a union like theirs
Would be a godsend for coastal cities
Highland towns   border villages

He wished them
Love always
Frequent silences
Long   sweetly-rebellious lives

And sat down

for Beth and Christian
August 27th 2005

Hunting
for Tom

After school in the fall
Kneeling with our bows
Behind those stone walls

We shot up at crows
Flapping across the fields
Never hitting one
Never in our heart of hearts hoping to

We knocked the ledges
With chunks of rock in our fists
Listening for that hollow sound
Of the tombs of braves
All the time unclear
About the meaning of finding true bones

In the woods we found three small ponds
Square-rimmed with flat chosen stones
Said to have been Indian ponds

The water in them choked with leaves
The October chill before dinner
Filled with vastness   a suffering

Plein Air

With ease these days   he sees himself
Walking off into the landscape
That hangs above the fireplace

White oaks in full leaf
Shadows draped over boulders
In the foreground grass

No commotion of crows this early
No trace of trespass
When he enters the scene

Just above the artist's signature
Entering in as ever
With the one he loves

Together past the red barn   red silo   red shed
Together through that opening
In the rail fence

Out along the edges of the plowed fields
Together past that speck-of-a-white-farmhouse
On the hill   until

Specks themselves
About to vanish into those green-blue
Slightly-impastoed woods

The two of them look back
Picturing the artist
Not far from his dilapidated car

Where tiger lilies trumpet the ditch
There on that little rise
Painting paradise

Touching a dipped brush
High up on his canvas now
Catching the billows and wisps

Of a fast-flying
Once-in-a-lifetime sky

5

River Millwork

for Eamon Grennan

A sea's mood swings
A bay's sweep
Seabirds   a sea's salt

Not hard to see
How the owners
Would imagine a window

In that plain gable end
And how the woodworker
Would sketch from the lawn

Climb the attic's pine winders
(An uprush of heat from the lower floors
A rapture of open rafters)

To take his dimensions
To picture the tracery in place   and through it
The early sun   the bridge

The far shore in fog
Stars
A sea-wind's shear and blown rain

After Dark

After dark
A wakefulness may come
Having little to do with sleeplessness

Or bells
Or vigils
Or lapidary inscriptions
Or old federations
Or mattresses stuffed with cash
Or doomsaying
Or orders of angels
Or predictions of snow enough this winter
To bury us all

Empty as we are
Praise may be easier

We may recognize ourselves
As otherworldly by nature

High fields in the moonlight
Swaying in summer air
Choiring up there in whispers

Vespers

Daylight draining when our farmer arrives
In his bashed-up dump truck

His daughter (14   maybe 15 now)
Steering their relic of a front-end loader

They wave as they drive
To the back of the shop

And through the scrape and heave
Of a month's worth of woodchips

Signal each other
The way road crews do

The way conductors call for
More choir   less brass

Their headlights ghosting the shale hill
Sweeping its broad stand of birches

Heaped and tarped now
They wave again

And diesel off down Hosler Road
Leaving me the incense

Of freshly-mined sawdust
Walnut   pine   oak   cherry

Leaving me low singing in the hollows
Darkness   stars   wide silence

A chill that will deepen overnight
And excavate

Its phantom machinery
Leveling the valleys with frost

Stopping Off

Union Cemetery
Slate Hill   New York

A chipmunk zigzags the tractor path

Sloping from the orchard

To the cemetery on the knoll

Where I've strayed this morning

On my way to town

To pick up hinges and primer

He fidgets through the balusters

Latticed in vine

Near an obelisk topped with a dove

Freezes there   the breeze gives me away I think

Squirts off between the pitched slabs

Over the face of an inscription

Does a quick soft shoe

From one side of the cross to the other

And scats through forsythia

Like a churchyard here

Absent the usual white wooden church

I walk through the low gates

Rusted in the open position

Across the grass   wet still
In need of a mow   out among stones
With familiar last names

(The road that runs past my shop
The farmstead with the sway-backed barn
Its fields filled with solar panels now
That blue sign on the bridge over the creek)

And in the newer section
My landlord's wife
Gone nine years this month
With his name and date of birth
Graved beside hers

I waved to him
Yesterday when he drove by
Hands at 10 and 2   mouth agape
Staring down South Plank Road

Ordinary Time

Afternoon   alone in the house
Water on the stove for tea
He sifts the mail   leafs a magazine
Known for its brainy humor
When   out of the blue (page 62)
There she is
One   O Lake of Fire
He'd 'sell his soul for'

Ah   he's always had a weakness
For the hyperbole of ecclesial clichés
Though   imagining her
As available as she looks in the ad
Hell, maybe 'sell his soul' is about right

As it was in the beginning
Those flickering first years of catechetical TV
Black and white   strictly 50's
Not a Doubting Thomas in the house
When on small screens from coast to coast
Fulton J. Sheen would miraculously appear
Like the Messiah Himself
Except with higher ratings

Remember the way
He'd call a spade a spade
His prime time flourishes
In strait-laced bishop's regalia

The way he'd hit his mark
And pick up chalk and spill it out
In billowy Catholic longhand
Con-cu-pi-scence dot dot dot

But now the sun slips in the west
The china moon scrims the blue air
Like a communion host

Ordinary time   Lord
A string of weeks with days of rest
From those old parochial ghosts

And all things being equal
It's heaven enough down here
Eden as is
Given God's wide water   blazing trees
Given the valley's coil and rise
Given woman curves (Amen)
As far as the eye can see

City Psalm

How to account
For the way she appears

Walking past the sun-splashed cathedral
Colossal window and all

How to offer some
Explanation for man

His masonry everywhere
Bells going off

Wounded by her movement
As she crosses Amsterdam

Can anybody with a body doubt
Her arms are evidence of things unseen

Isn't she temple enough
And proof

That One who frescoes
Afternoons as blue as this

Can lift up metropolitan dust
Glory be

She walks west
And sets flesh singing

And the street signs sing
And the river breeze sings

Even the old stone saints
Shadowed   open-mouthed

Barnacled to the great
Carved archways are tempted

To pick up instruments
And shout out the good news as she goes

Sunday

Early over the footbridge
Up cemetery hills
Early treading the logging road's steady rise
Out of the self

Stumped   leaf-littered
Peppered with fallen limbs
Its ruts clumped with deer grass
Verge loose with laurel

Roses riot in an unfarmed field
A rock fence tumbles the undergrowth
A clear-cut shimmers with birch

Sunday
And looking from a ledge
Above steeples   fire lines   washouts   ravines
River silvering through the valley

Good
The way daylight bathes
The miniature town below

The way shale paths discontinue
The way spirit awakens in skin
As a breeze lifts scotch pine and cedar

Good
Red bird on a rhododendron
Water   pooling   releasing
Sluicing stones of every transgression

Open Water

The diesel-brine-fish smell
Of the port drifts off

And from the deck
The docks

Lobster pots heaped up
Massive rope   colored flags

All shrink from view
While the sun trails overhead

Sea Level

He gets out
From under the weight of the wood

No soul music
No drums now to delay him

No dry homily as the turnpike
Becomes a two-lane alternate
Becomes a shore road
That threads the marshland
And dead-ends without notice in sand

Sea level   stars risen
Where the bay slow-rolls the beach
Where a buoy clangs beyond the jetty
Where boulders older than Gethsemane
Cloister in the coastal air

Lights flare the long harbor
Where for all he knows
He might have lived another life once

Acknowledgments

Grateful thanks to Eamon Grennan for helping me to 'remove the scaffolding,' and for lending so generously to this collection his Irish ear and eye.

To *The Recorder*, literary journal of the American Irish Historical Society, for publishing 'River Millwork' (in an earlier version).

To *Poetry on the Loose*, at which a number of the poems in this book were first presented.

To Priscilla Orr, Sussex County Community College, for asking me to design and present the workshop called *Brushstrokes*, for which the poem 'Preamble' was written.

Thanks to local publications that published poems in this book: *The Journal, Pike County Dispatch, Pike County Courier.*

About The Author

Chuck O'Neil has written five poetry collections, most recently *better gods*. He lives in Milford, Pennsylvania, where he and his wife, Celeste, have lived since 1982. They have four children and three grandchildren. In 2022 he was named Poet Laureate of Milford.

Photo by Marie Liu

www.chuckoneilauthor.com